Praise for *Until the Flood*

"In this current moment of extraordinary discord in American society, Dael Orlandersmith's *Until the Flood* offers a heartrending demonstration of the potential of art to reach across cultural boundaries and generate the kind of empathy that could potentially help bring us all closer together . . . Part of the appeal of *Until the Flood* lies in seeing the dazzlingly nimble ways in which Orlandersmith transforms from one character to another—throwing a chair out of frustration and crying for blood in one moment, becoming a mild-mannered teacher the next . . . When, in the show's final minutes, Orlandersmith herself finally speaks in her own voice to articulate her own sorrowful yet hopeful perspective, the effect is akin to that of a prayer, a poetic plea for understanding and peace that ought to be heard all across the land."

—*TheaterMania*

"Deeply humane . . . A moving and important piece."

—*London Evening Standard*

"Quietly devastating . . . The picture Orlandersmith paints isn't of an isolated eruption following a single tragic incident, but something much more ominous—a society riven by deep, perhaps insurmountable cracks. Whether or not there is any hope, it is a salve to see that beauty can arise from such tragedy . . . Fascinating, moving."

—*Time Out London*

"Orlandersmith crafts a stunning theatrical experience that must be seen."

—*Portland Observer*

UNTIL THE FLOOD

A Play

DAEL ORLANDERSMITH

THEATRE COMMUNICATIONS GROUP
NEW YORK
2019

The publication of *Until the Flood* by Dael Orlandersmith, through TCG's Book Program, is made possible in part by the New York State Council on the Arts with the support of Governor Andrew Cuomo and the New York State Legislature.

TCG books are exclusively distributed to the book trade by Consortium Book Sales and Distribution.

Library of Congress Control Numbers:
2019020723 (print) / 2019022351 (ebook)
ISBN 978-1-55936-596-3 (paperback) / ISBN 978-1-55936-909-1 (ebook)
A catalog record for this book is available from the Library of Congress.

Book design and composition by Lisa Govan
Cover design by Rodrigo Corral
Author photo by Tess Mayer

First Edition, December 2019

*Dedicated to Ferguson
and world healing*

CONTENTS

Until the Flood was written and performed by Dael Orlandersmith.

Until the Flood was commissioned by and received its world premiere at The Repertory Theatre of St. Louis (Steven Woolf, Artistic Director; Mark Bernstein, Managing Director) in St. Louis, Missouri, on October 12, 2016. It was directed by Neel Keller. The scenic design was by Takeshi Kata, the costume design was by Kaye Voyce, the lighting design was by Mary Louise Geiger, the sound design was by Justin Ellington; the projection designer was Nicholas Hussong, and the production stage manager was Tony Dearing.

Until the Flood received its New York premiere at Rattlestick Playwrights Theater (Daniella Topol, Artistic Director; Annie Middleton, Managing Director) in New York City on January 6, 2018. The artistic team remained the same, except the production stage manager was Laura Wilson.

Until the Flood was produced by Milwaukee Repertory Theater (Mark Clements, Artistic Director; Chad Bauman, Executive Director) in Milwaukee, Wisconsin, on March 13, 2018. The artistic team remained the same, except the production stage manager was Sarah Deming-Henes.

Until the Flood was produced by the Goodman Theatre (Robert Falls, Artistic Director; Roche Schulfer, Executive Director) in

Chicago, Illinois, on April 26, 2018. The artistic team remained the same, except the production stage manager was Angela M. Adams.

Until the Flood was produced by ACT Theatre (John Langs, Artistic Director; Becky Witmer, Managing Director) in Seattle, Washington, on June 8, 2018. The artistic team remained the same, except the production stage manager was Erin B. Zatloka.

Until the Flood was produced by Portland Center Stage at the Armory (Marissa Wolf, Artistic Director; Cynthia Fuhrman, Managing Director) in Portland, Oregon, on March 16, 2019. The artistic team remained the same, except the production stage manager was Kristen Mun.

Until the Flood received its European premiere in a production by the Arcola Theatre (Mehmet Ergen, Artistic Director; Leyla Nazli, Executive Producer; Ben Todd, Executive Director; Jack Gamble, Associate Director; Richard Speir, Producer) at the Galway International Arts Festival in Galway, Ireland, on July 22, 2019. The artistic team was the same as the original production. The Arcola production then transferred to the Traverse Theatre in Edinburgh, Scotland, on August 1, 2019; and to the Arcola Theatre in London, England, on September 4, 2019. The artistic team remained the same, except the production stage manager was Kenzie Murray, and with the addition of Geoff Hense as production coordinator.

A new play based on interviews
conducted in St. Louis in spring 2015.

This play can be performed as
single character, multi-character;
any race, age, or gender.

LOUISA

Part One

Louisa Hemphill, black, early seventies, retired schoolteacher. Talks to audience:

LOUISA

It was a nice service / real nice / that preacher really went at it didn't he? He sweated—the way he sweated—real old school. I happen to like that though—the old-school preaching.

(Beat.)

The way he spoke about that boy's death Michael Brown and all the stuff happening in Ferguson didn't surprise me a bit. That whole race thing—that was a long time coming.

(Louisa sips tea.)

Back then when I was a young girl—no black policeman same as now . . . isn't that something?

I mean if you were standing outside of your OWN home talking to somebody—they'd yell at you: *(Does a voice)* "Get inside." . . . I mean you're on your own property . . . or they'd pull black men over for no reason.

(Beat.)

It was always like that . . . cops doing that or white boys / these crazy / insane white boys in cars / drunk/sober looking for trouble / looking for something to Do / speeding past yelling out "NIGGER" . . . looking for something to do . . . my god.

And

Of course they—the whites—were protected by the law—especially the "sundown law."

If you don't know what that is . . . it was a law / AWFUL law that stated if you were of color or Jewish you could not be in certain towns after dark.

There were those signs: *(As if reading a sign)* "Don't let the sun go down on you in this town nigger."

(Pause. Back to audience:)

We all saw those signs

Read those signs

Saw those signs

(Pause.)

I saw those signs

There were those of us who did indeed abide by that law

And

Who lived by that law

But

Those signs angered me

Really angered me

And

I showed how it angered me

Spoke about it

Sometimes yelled about it

My family would hear me out

They understood

But

It seemed to me that they took IT

Took "keeping their place."

It seemed to me that my family were passive racially

My father seemed like a man who did not "outstep his bounds."

There was THAT racism as well.

Certainly there was the violence

But

There was also the UNDERSTOOD / quiet racism that did NOT include violence

Everyone knew their "place."

The whites stayed in West County

And

We stayed in Kinloch back then and later Ferguson.

If we had to go shopping say in Normandy—it was understood we were there for JUST that / and the white folk there knew us by name and we knew them by name and smiles and even some conversation was had.

BUT

Then it was back to Kinloch

Back there before the sun went down

Back to OUR side of town

And

THEIR side of town

Back to keeping your place.

(Pause.)

I would NOT: *(Sarcastically)* "keep my place." / I refused to "KEEP MY PLACE."

(Beat.)

I graduated high school and went to City College in New York

By then it was the sixties

And

there were no race riots in St. Louis period

But

when I was in New York

I went to protests

I participated in boycotts

And

heard about the race riots in Chicago and Indiana—THOSE riots—
my god! . . . put fire in ME

Yes

I was on FIRE.

(Pause.)

Sometimes when I came home to visit / I'd sense a hostility

Not with my family but from certain WHITE and BLACK people

There was a HATRED directed towards ME

Once I was in a store in Normandy to get my mother some fabric.

And

Again the woman—a white woman—I knew her all my life—Mrs. Wexton was one of the folk my family made small talk with when they came into her shop.

So this day I came in and by then it was 1969-70—and she said: *(Does her)* "Oh Louisa! Haven't seen you in such a long time."

(Becomes self:)

And I say: *(As if to her)* "Well Mrs. Wexton, I've been living in New York studying at City College."

(Pause. Back to audience:)

And

Suddenly her face dropped

It just DROPPED

And

She said: *(Does her)* "Another one."

(Becomes self:)

And

Then I said: *(As if to her)* "Ma'am? . . ."

(Becomes self:)

And she says: *(Does her)* "All the colored folk—sorry or should I say BLACK—'cause all of you are BLACK now—ALL the blacks are going to Chicago or New York—forgetting where they come from. Maybe it's better you leave, that way you won't be causing any trouble HERE."

(Becomes self:)

I looked at her in disbelief and again said: *(As if to her)* "MA'AM?"

(Back to audience:)

I then said: *(As if to her)* "Mrs. Wexton / I change my mind / I don't want to buy anything from your store."

(Back to audience:)

I turned around and walked out.

(Beat.)

Her mouth fell open

But

What stays with me is the black girl that worked for her.

(Beat.)

As Mrs. Wexton and I had this exchange / there was a black girl about my age sweeping the floor and putting things away.

And

When I told Mrs. Wexton about my being in New York and attending college / the girl looked at me

We were about the same age

She looked at me HARD

She looked at me saying without saying: *(Does a voice)* "You think you're better than me? You think 'cause you went east / talk different that you're better than me?"

(Pause. Becomes self:)

And

As

Mrs. Wexton called herself telling me off / the girl was smirking.

There was a smirk on her face as if to say: *(Does a voice)* "That's what you get for not keeping your place / that's JUST what you get."

(Pause. Becomes self:)

In that moment / I was filled with HATE

I was filled with hatred for her—THAT BLACK Girl

And

She HATED ME.

(Beat. Speaks quietly:)

I drove back home

And

I told my family what happened

My father looked at me and said: *(Does him)* "Louisa, you should feel sorry for her / I know who she is / I know her family / you should feel bad for her . . ."

(Beat. Becomes self:)

Then

I raved

I raved and said: *(As if speaking to father)* "That girl got mad at ME because I wasn't cleaning Mrs. Wexton's floor / she's a TOM and I can't believe you're defending her."

(Becomes self:)

And

Again my father said: *(Does father's voice)* "Louisa, sometimes YOU can know so much and yet know so little."

(Becomes self:)

And

When

he said that I was livid / I said: *(As if to him)* "THAT GIRL IS A TOM, DAD / AND YOU DEFENDING HER MAKES YOU A TOM—"

(Becomes self:)

And before I could finish my sentence / my mother pushed my father aside

And

She slapped me

She slapped me palm to face

And

Back hand to face saying: *(Does mother's voice)* "DON'T you EVER call your father that / EVER / the reason why you're ALIVE and have the education that you have is because he's STRONG. / IF you feel that he's a TOM / then you leave this house and NEVER COME BACK."

(Pause. Becomes self:)

I held my tears

But

I couldn't totally hold them

Some of them did spill.

(Pause.)

I looked into my father's eyes

And

The hurt that was there . . . *(Voice trails off)*

(Beat.)

It wasn't until I reached my mid-to-late thirties and moved back to St. Louis

And

when

BOTH parents died / I realized

SAW

And I remember my father saying how racism causes SELF-hate.

(Beat.)

LEGACY is the word that comes to mind—LEGACY.

The legacy of self-hate.

The legacy of "keeping your place."

The legacy of "grinning and bowing."

The legacy of seeing yourself as a NIGGER. / Being taught to see yourself as a NIGGER.

(Pause.)

My god how I hate that word

How I hate when ANYBODY—white or black—uses it.

(Beat.)

That young man

Michael Brown—his death. He was made to see himself that way

As a NIGGER

As someone who was nondeserving

He was set up and set himself up to fail

To steal tiparillos of all things— WHY?

What purpose?

HE graduated high school / was about to enter college in the fall?

What made him do that?

WHO made him do that?

I'm ANGRY at HIM.

(Pause.)

I'm just angry in general.

(The lights fade on Louisa.)

RUSTY

The lights come up on Rusty Harden: seventy-five, white, retired police-man, lives in Lemay. Talks to audience:

RUSTY

I lived in Lemay all my life / I got family that goes back three generations here and most people can claim that same thing because we're all similar. *(Pause)* All of us are white and there's nothing wrong with that. *(Pause)* Just 'cause I'm PRO-white doesn't mean I'm ANTI-anybody else. *(Beat)* . . . My dad's people were English and my mother's people were Swedes. My dad's people settled here— Don't know the whole story but again from the north of England and they came here because where they were in the north there were tons of farmers and they decided to come to a place where they could prosper and not have much competition . . . at least that was the story I heard . . .

(Beat.)

I love Missouri—I live in and can't see myself living any other place . . . I've seen other places—visited some other places but ALL I care about / need is right here . . .

All my family, friends, comforts—HERE.

(Beat.)

I was a policeman—retired seventeen years ago . . . / I worked in Ferguson there and saw the changes . . . it was back in the sixties an' seventies nice—quiet, mostly white . . .

I worked the force from 1969–1999 . . . thirty years . . . A few of the policemen lived in Ferguson but worked in Kinloch and then later moved to Mehlville, Lemay or farther out to Arnold.

A lot of them moved to Crestwood.

(Pause.)

That's where Darren Wilson lives.

(Beat.)

Kinloch was black and there were NO blacks on the force . . . *(Pause)* I didn't see a problem with that / if someone is capable of doing the job—it doesn't matter.

(Emphatic:)

If there is a true respect for the law—does not matter—not at all— If someone can carry out the law—then that's a GOOD THING.

BUT If someone cannot carry out the law / they got no business in this line of work / I mean a gun is a powerful thing / a person's life is important and if somebody doesn't know that / can't see past that . . .

(Pause.)

That's a dangerous dangerous man . . . the man who can't see past that . . .

(Beat.)

I've had to raise my gun a few times

And

I see the faces sometimes of men I've had to use the gun on

The suspect is yelling at you calling you "WHITE TRASH / HONKY" and a crowd gathers and they ALL start to chant/yell and someone in that crowd just sees a white man with a gun . . . and every racial thing that EVER happened in that moment to them or what they think happened to them / that white man will be on the receiving end of ALL of it. —This ALWAYS happens and they will NOW yell WHITE TRASH/HONKY super loud. And they surround you and dare you to shoot—they stand before you KNOWING the gun is loaded—daring you to shoot and the look on that person's face / those people's faces are: "I don't care about dying / I just don't care and I'll take you with me."

THAT is the look on their faces / that person's face

Not caring about living

Not CARING

I mean They KNOW by trying to kill you or killing you / they could lose their life.

It's like THEY WANT to die

So

you HAVE to use your gun

When somebody has nothing to lose / you gotta use your gun

And

Within SECONDS you're dealing with LIFE

You have to watch how that person can reach for their gun

If THEY know guns well

How fast are THEY moving?

What is that person's intention?

Can you talk the person down?

Can you reason with this person?

You see their fear / anger

You're dealing with YOUR OWN fear / anger.

(Pause.)

THEN

you better use your gun

You BETTER use it

That is not a BLACK person

That is a NIGGER.

(Beat.)

My son said to me / said: *(Does him)* "Dad even if the person is a BAD black person, isn't it the job of the law to really try and work with that person and only use the gun as a LAST resort?"

(Beat. Becomes self:)

I understand what he's saying but I also got mad. REAL mad—this is an oversimplification.

(Suddenly defensive:)

Look I know how things can be

I know there should have been some blacks on the force

I CAN see that

But

I ALSO say if a cop is a good man—what difference does the color make?

(Beat.)

You put your life on the line for people

You risk your life

You're out there

I'm not gonna go against a brother

And

When I say "brother"—black or white—I mean a cop

A cop is a brother.

(Pause.)

I wasn't there when Darren used his gun

And

The people that were there

Some lie

Some tell the truth

And

Then

There is the combo of BOTH

And

Some just wanna jump to get some publicity.

People can be like that you know.

(Beat.)

I Do search my own soul

I do it ALL the time

I can get lost in the past

Sometimes I can drink a little too much whiskey—I'm the first one to tell you that.

Sometimes I want the feelings to float away

Wash away.

(Pause.)

I do feel for Michael Brown

And

His family

And

I feel for Darren Wilson

My son may not believe it but I FEEL

I DO feel . . .

(Pause.)

I wasn't there when—Darren—my BROTHER used his gun

Felt he had to use his gun

I wasn't there

And

Neither was my son.

(Pause.)

Neither one of us was

My son wasn't there

I wasn't there

He doesn't know

I don't know

We weren't there

Neither one of us know

We just don't know.

(Pause.)

It's about going with the tide

Goin with the flow

You just gotta go with the flow.

(The lights fade on Rusty.)

HASSAN

The lights come up on Hassan Black: seventeen; street kid; speaks in a regular, poetic, aggressive voice. Talks to audience:

HASSAN

Today man—today I just DON'T CARE. Feel me?

I don't care about nothing or nobody

I'm a fluid nigga

Ya feel me

I do it fluid

Slow St. Louis/Mississippi flow

River.

(Pause.)

Nigga

Slow / flow nigga

Like when I'm rappin to a girl

Kickin it to her

And

She can hear my flow

And

She knows she like it

But

Pretends she don't

Pretends to throw me shade

But

At the end—my flow wins

'Cuz

I'm fluid

I do it fluid.

(Beat.)

My moms was fightin with her boyfriend today—shit was ugly yo

So

I wanted to get out of Ferguson

And

Cruise.

(Pause.)

So I find my boys

And

One of em's got a car

And

We're riding

Ya feel me?

And

We see Po-lice

All white PO-lice

yeah / yeah / yeah like them po-lice fuckin wit niggas . . . know what
I'm sayin? . . . like I'ma tell U / they fuck wit nigga for no reason

Me an my boys were Crusin / we was goin a little fast

Not real fast

Just a little

Kickin it

You feel me?

Just kickin it

And

Po-lice stopped us

Pulled out they guns

Made us ALL get out of the car

And

Gave my boy—my boy who was drivin a hundred-dollar fine

And

He says: "Officer I wasn't goin that fast."

And

The Po-lice said: "Want me to add another hundred?"

And

I said to my boy: "Yo be cool man / don't say nothin else."

And

I looked at this South Side–livin cracker knowin that a hundred dollars ain't shit to him

But

It's a lot for US

And

All he had to do was to tell us to stop

He didn't have to pull his gun

All we was doin was cruisin a little too fast

And

And

Maybe playin music a little too loud

But

That was all

He didn't have to pull no gun

And

He was HUNGRY man

Motherfucker was hungry to shoot a nigga

And

I looked back at him sayin with my eyes: "Yeah do it / do it mutha-fucka!"

And

He looked back at me / his finger on the trigger

Droolin

Like a dog mutt

Just like a hungry dog mutt

I bet Mike Brown saw that too

Saw Po-lice lookin HUNGRY

Just like a hungry dog mutt.

(As if to him:)

Right Mike?

(Beat. Back to audience:)

We drove around

We drove over to U City

Clayton

And

Then to Webster Grove

I wanted to see where you were going to make this play

We drove to the St. Louis Repertory

I don't know why but I was just looking at thinking how I never seen a play before

I want to

I never been to a theater before and I want to go.

(Pause.)

I was thinking about how maybe I could write a play

Do somethin like that

Write a play and have the whole play be in flow

A play of rap/flow.

(Pause.)

Then

We cruised through Crestwood

We wanted to see Crestwood

We wanted to see were Darren Wilson lived.

(Pause.)

I WANTED to see how he lived

What kind of hood it was—you know

Like how does he LIVE man?

Like

Was it clean?

The street he lived on

Was it clean?

We didn't know what street he lived on

We thought we could drive there

And

Find his house.

(Pause.)

I wanted to look him in the eye

I wanted to see what he looked like up close

In the flesh

Him and me

I wanted to see if he would pull his gun on ME

I wanted to see if I would be scared of him

I wanted to see if I would make the first move

Front like I had a gun

And

I wondered if he'd shoot me

And

Then another part of me was sayin: "Why would you wanna do that man? . . . Front like you got a gun? . . ."

I wonder why I was thinkin that?

Thinkin like this

All fluid / like water man

Just comin man

Like the river—ya feel me?

All these thoughts . . .

(Beat.)

I ain't know Mike Brown

Him and me had niggas in common

But

I ain't know him

But I find myself talking to him

Talking to him NOW

After he's gone

I wonder why I keep doin that.

(Beat.)

And

In Ferguson

I see that memorial spot they got for Michael Brown every day

Every day I see it

And

I want to CRUISE somewhere

Be

SOMEWHERE

I just wanna cruise

CRUISE outta here—PERIOD.

(Beat.)

Anytime we Cruise / I really take in the houses

I look at nice houses we pass as we cruise

I'm thinkin of the houses in U City

I'm thinkin how nice those houses are

Thinkin how quiet it is

Thinkin how clean it is

All them rich white people

Thinkin Berkeley is clean too

Rich niggas in Berkeley

Thinkin of dem rich niggas lucky to be rich.

(Beat.)

I'm thinkin of my teacher

History teacher

He's black

One of the few black people in Clayton

And

He's married with two kids

And

How he said to me: *(Does him)* "Hassan you are smart and if you apply yourself you can go far and I ALSO know you are a GOOD person / I wish you could believe that / that you're smart and GOOD."

(Becomes self:)

I wanted to cry

Wanted to say to him:

(Pause. As if to his teacher:)

"Take me home wit you / I want you to be my father."

(Pause. Back to audience:)

And

I was thinking how it would be to have him as my father

And

I was thinkin about how it would be to live in Clayton

And

I'm thinking of the kids that have parents / have BOTH parents

BOTH parents MARRIED

And

BOTH parents carin about them.

(Pause.)

Lovin them

Tonight I'm feelin it

Feelin like kickin it

Kickin some ass

And

I don't care about nothin

And

I DO know right from wrong

I DO know

But

I'm mad

I'm mad / crazy

And

I mad / ANGRY

And

I don't CARE

You feel me

I just DON'T CARE

Anger man

My Anger is FLUID

And

I bet Mike Mike musta felt it too

I mean I Know he did.

(As if to him:)

"Yo Mike I KNOW you did."

(Pause. Back to audience:)

I want to smash somethin

Fuck it up

Fuck somebody up!

And

There are days I don't care

And

TODAY is one them days

And

I feel like I am in a DAZE

'Cuz

I know I can't make it

I can't

And

there is A PART OF ME that wants to go

Get out

there is That part WANTS to stand before a GUN

Right in front of some redneck hungry motherfucker

Some redneck motherfucker who don't know my name

Don't care what my name is

But

I know this motherfucker would aim to shoot

and

NOT MISS.

(Pause.)

I'm seventeen man

Sometimes I feel seven

Sometimes I feel seventy

And

I want

Out

Spill my BLOOD MAN

SPILL IT!

(Brings finger to his head as if it were a gun. Pause.)

I

Just

Want

OUT

DO IT!

DO IT FLUID!

(The lights fade on Hassan.)

CONNIE

The lights come up on Connie Hamm: white, thirty-five, a high school teacher who lives and works in University City. Talks to audience:

CONNIE

I have been following the case—Michael Brown—although I live and work in University City—I teach at the university—

(Beat.)

I rarely go to Ferguson but this lovely wine bar here . . .

It seems so strange to have this wine bar here

But

I'm glad it's here—really glad

I see all kinds of people in here

It's kind of an oasis from all the tension / if only for a little while

A nice place where we can tranquilize ourselves—if only for a little while.

(Beat.)

The Michael Brown shooting—I really think it's tragic on so many levels . . . I think of the tragedy of BOTH young men . . .

I think really—well again I can't speak for anyone and I as a white person DEFINITELY can't speak to what it's like for a person of color.

(Pause.)

In "U City"—people call it—people are mostly white and they speak about it in a very detached way.

You hear people swallowing their coffee and right after / they say: "It's all so sad."

Then

they reach for a roll and butter and jelly for the roll and end the conversation with a shrug and: "Aw well / too bad . . ."

(Beat.)

I have a friend named Margaret and she's a schoolteacher . . . She used to teach at Normandy High in Normandy and / I hear she's moving to Chicago to teach at DePaul University—good for her . . .

(Pause.)

I know Margaret because sometimes there were meetings with other district schools where we would all meet to discuss and compare notes about teaching methods and race relations and how to reach ALL kids in general . . .

She and I got along very well and we both had similar views about having classes be racially mixed and how we must expand the program to include black history for instance . . .

We have gone to each other's houses for dinner

We've talked for hours on the phone—not just about school

We also spoke about our lives

The conversation between us flowed.

(Pause.)

We were FRIENDS talking about our lives

We'd sit here, drink wine and just tell each other stuff

I told her things I never told another soul

About my failed marriage

Divorce

How I left because my husband was abusive

But

No one would believe me because he was so WHITE and upstanding

Someone actually said that to me: *(Does a voice)* "He's white and well-to-do—why would he be violent? I Don't believe you!"

(Pause. Becomes self:)

My father was also abusive to my mother

My sister and I would watch him just haul off and slap her for no reason

And

Then he would beat us

But:

(Sarcastically:)

He was a chemical engineer.

(Beat.)

In other words I KNOW and understand violence

Abuse

I know what can happen.

(Beat.)

The death of Michael Brown is horrific . . . the ANGER he knew all his life from being mistreated and Darren Wilson . . .

And

I read about Darren Wilson and his background

THEIR fear

I believe they BOTH were afraid

What happened to THEM as kids?

BOTH lives are tragic

BOTH

And

Yeah maybe I sound naive but this is what I feel

Race affects EVERYONE

And

When Margaret and I would get together / she would look at me hard if I brought up the shooting.

(Beat.)

I was here at the wine bar and on my way home saw some white protesters. I saw Margaret the next day and told her about the white protesters and again started to say how tragic BOTH lives were

But

Before I could finish / she yelled: *(Does her)* "Look Connie— Michael Brown is dead and that Bastard Darren Wilson is alive . . . how is Darren Wilson tragic? That WHITE Bastard gunned down a black child / and HIS life is tragic? MY god! How I hate liberals. / At least with an out-and-out bigot I know where the hell I stand!"

(Becomes self:)

And I said: *(As if to her)* "Look Michael Brown should not have sto-
len and he should not have come after Darren Wilson—IF that's
what happened—and Darren Wilson should have exercised more
control / his using the gun should have been the LAST resort but
IF he HAD to use the gun—REALLY had to reach for it / he DID
have the right to defend himself and yes I do believe after seeing
footage of him that there IS some remorse / I believe that he has a
hard time living with what he's done."

(Becomes self:)

And

She looked me up and down

Walked off.

(Pause.)

I called after that

None of the calls were returned

I sent cards / emails

She didn't answer any of them . . . *(Voice trails off)*

(Beat.)

I really wish her well

I think it's great she got the teaching job in Chicago

She works hard

And

Totally deserves that job

That job SHOULD be hers and hers alone.

(Pause.)

I wish I could tell her that

Tell her that I really wish her well

I really wish I could tell her that I'll miss her

I'll miss having wine with her.

(Pause.)

I really wish I could.

(The lights fade on Connie.)

REUBEN

The lights come up on Reuben Little: black, late sixties/early seventies. He is in his barbershop in North City. He's cleaning scissors, combs. Talks to audience:

REUBEN

The thing is that you can't go by appearances—you really can't / I ought to know because I deal with people's appearance all the time working in a barbershop . . .

You know it's amazing what people tell you in barbershops and beauty parlors . . . really is . . . some of the stuff people tell me you wouldn't believe . . .

You hear about affairs people had or are having / stuff about kids and the wife . . .

Liquor / drug problems . . . all of it

I wonder why that is?

Why when folks sit in this chair *(Points to the chair)* they talk this way? . . . *(Slight pause)* I think maybe it's about not having to cover up for the moment.

In that moment / they're not having to LOOK a certain way

they're looking/feeling relaxed

They're not being judged

Because

We DO judge people based on Looks.

(Pause.)

That has happened to me ALL my life

And

Of course this also means race . . .

It's a GIVEN that you're judged on race.

(Pause.)

And

Yeah we've all been talking about the Michael Brown case

You hear all kinds of stuff

The guys get in the chair or they come in and it's been a hot topic to say the least.

I care about BLACK folks being treated fairly

The system does NOT treat us fairly

I don't want preferential treatment

I just want my right as a hardworking, honest man like my white counterpart

That's EVERYBODY'S right

And

Yeah I would love to know what the TRUTH is in reference to Michael Brown.

(Beat.)

You know these two young girls / two writers—students from Northwestern came here to the shop to write about the Michael Brown case

One was black

And

The other one was white

And

(Wryly:)

Both of them were very GREEN till it came to their questions

Anyway they came here to MY barbershop

One of my regulars Sonny somehow met them

And

Led them here to me.

(Pause. Wryly:)

Knowing Sonny he probably was trying—as we used to say / back in the day—"get next to them" because both of them are pretty.

(Beat.)

Anyway these girls came in

And

Sonny and a few of the guys were sitting here / hanging around like usual

And

They—these girls came in, came in saying how they wanted to write about this case and: *(Does a voice)* "Show the HORRORS of racism and poverty and how Michael Brown was a 'victim.'" And the black girl—angry—radical said that: *(Does her)* "ALL black people are VICTIMS."

(Becomes self:)

And

I looked at her

Really looked at her

And

I knew this girl came from Privilege

Smooth life.

"Easy flow" I call it.

I could see that she really wasn't raised around a lot black folk

Or

At least poor / lower-class black folk

And

I could tell the white one came from a well-to-do—

Probably the only black folks she ever came across were the ones that cleaned her family's house

But

She was trying to understand.

(Pause. Wryly:)

And

Having said that / maybe I'm wrong

I mean I could be wrong now!

I can be wrong just like anybody else!

That's what I mean when I say how people judge you on how you look.

(Semi-long pause:)

BUT

I KNOW I'M NOT

And

These two girls

The green Black Girl

And

The green White Girl did that with ME

And

Sonny and all the guys

It was like in a way they WANTED us to be Victims

THEY were looking to "SAVE US" . . .

And

They

They were nice girls but . . . *(Voice trails off)*

(Beat.)

They came in the shop / looked around and said: *(Does a voice)* "Mr. Little I see how hard it is for you to carve out a living here in North City / it's been made hard for you."

(Becomes self:)

And

I said to them: "First off call me Reuben and second of all I'm doing fine. Today is slow but I do make a living and a GOOD one, ladies."

(Back to audience:)

And

And

The green Black one said: *(Does her)* "Well you're really great and I see how you make yourself see the good in what you do and you don't allow yourself to be looked down upon the way Michael Brown and his family was looked down upon."

(Becomes self:)

Then

The green White one said: *(Does her)* "Michael Brown's murder and the murder of nine black men this year symbolizes the EMO-TIONAL and MENTAL strife that you, Reuben, and all blacks have had to suffer historically and we want to write about that and SPLASH it over every magazine / every NEWS program we can."

(Becomes self:)

And

I looked at Sonny and all the guys

And

They looked back at me and kinda rolled their eyes.

And

I looked at BOTH of these green women

And

I said to both of them: *(Speaking to them)* "Young ladies, just so you know, I am Not a Victim. I live here in North City because I choose to and in reference to this shop, the shop is MINE and this building in fact is MINE and I have tenants upstairs I rent to . . . I attended Tuskegee College and came back here because I WANTED TO / I cut hair because I WANT TO and I ENJOY IT / I learn about human nature in ways / many ways people don't.

What bothers me is how many people assume that BLACK folks who come from a poor background are innately intellectually inferior. I really wish people would look at the Historical ramifications of race and how that affects people psychologically as well . . . the fact that you're told you're not intelligent enough—that you're intellectually inferior because of RACE—does a number on your head and SOUL.

I have had of course the racists call me NIGGER

And

Say the ONLY thing I'm good for is cutting hair or some such rot

But

At least with a racist / I know EXACTLY how I stand

It's the others that bother me

Like

the white do-gooders come under the guise of Liberalism trying to 'HELP' me because they felt I couldn't possibly stand on my own two feet

Again race and Appearances . . .

And

Now the both of YOU come making some of those same assumptions and I find it highly insulting—insulting to all of us here."

(Beat. Continues to speak to the girls:)

"But for you—well-intentioned or not—to come to me or ANY BLACK man and make it sound like we're victims / coming in with your ROMANTIC notion about saving me—and the other MEN sitting in this shop and other black men—by using the Michael Brown case in this way means you have taken on the very Bigotry you claim to despise.

Black men are not children / I am Not a child

I don't need you to DEFEND ME

I don't need you to SPEAK for me

Strong blood flows in my veins

I want MY FAIR due

And

Again

Michael Brown's family should have THEIR FAIR due

Darren Wilson should have HIS FAIR due

Don't judge ME by appearances or any of us thinking that you KNOW us so well

The Both of you know nothing

Nothing at all."

(Pause. Back to audience:)

And

Indeed

The both of them were close to tears

Sonny said: *(Does him)* "Reub, give the girls a break."

(Becomes self:)

And

I said: *(To Sonny)* "I gave them the TRUTH. We don't need to be infantilized, man."

(Back to audience:)

They got up, mumbled a "thank you"

And

Left

The guys—with the exception of Sonny—said I was right

And

They looked at me

And

Winked and said: *(Does a voice)* "Thanks Reuben."

(Pause. Becomes self:)

It's not about appearances / not all

Can't always judge

Good man

Thug

Whatever you want to call him—Michael

Or me

Or anyone else

It's about being FAIR

About FAIRNESS

THAT'S what it's about

Not Appearances.

It's not about appearances at all.

(The lights fade on Reuben.)

DOUGRAY

The lights come up on Dougray Smith: white, late thirties/early forties, land owner and electrician, lives in Tower Grove South. Talks to audience:

DOUGRAY

I don't come from much / not much at all.

But

I made something of myself

I live here in America—the greatest country in the world

And

I don't care what ANYBODY says / if you like the song says "straighten up and fly right"—you'll do fine

JUST Fine

That whole Michael Brown thing . . . *(Voice trails off)*

(Beat.)

I mean if it's so bad here / then why do so many people want to come here?

If America is so racist and unjust—why are there so many immigrants.

(Beat.)

Like I said / I come from NOTHING

I do NOT come from privilege

Contrary to popular belief not all white people come from privilege.

By that what I mean is that no one ever gave me anything and the people I was born to / raised by are basically white trash . . . *(Pause)* I know how that may sound insensitive to some people but it's true . . .

I was born and raised in the rough part of Charleston, West Virginia, and that whole hillbilly / moonshine thing was there and is still there and my family was and still IS a part of that . . .

The typical fighting / getting drunk / young girls having babies real early and people taking drugs like heroin and even more recently crystal meth is there now more than ever . . .

(Beat.)

I hated living like that

I hated it

And

My family hated ME for not being like them.

(Beat.)

I loved books / still love books

Hemingway's *A Moveable Feast* is my favorite book

I would not drop out of school

I would not run moonshine

Or

Sell dope

I rarely dated and of course got called "queer"

But . . .

(He smiles. The smile is almost sinister.)

If someone got in my face / if someone came at me physically—it was TOTAL WAR

TOTAL

I learned real early how to defend myself—real early.

(Beat.)

My father was one brutal man—brutal

He was a drunk

Both he and my mother were drunks

He Could never hold down a job

Beat my mother / me / my siblings

But

One day I rose up

I just rose.

(Pause.)

He came home drunk again this one night

We all listened for his walk

If we heard him bumping into stuff in the yard

Or

On the porch / we knew he was drunk

Well this night / I was reading . . .

Reading as usual

This night I was reading F. Scott Fitzgerald's *Tender Is the Night* at the supper table

And

He came in and snatched the book out of my hand

And

He snarled: *(Does him)* "Gonna burn this book / gonna burn it boy."

(Becomes self:)

And

He snatched the book from my hands

And

He went towards the stove

Staggering

Laughing

Holding the book in the air—he was a big man—6'4" he was

And

Even though I was seventeen and about 5'10" I couldn't reach it

And

He was laughing

Shoving me back

Saying: *(Does him)* "GONNA Burn this book QUEER Bastard / GONNA BURN IT."

(Becomes self:)

And

He goes over to the stove and turns on one of the burners

And

Holds the book over it

And

The book goes on fire

And

I pick up a chair

And

I hit him with it

I just slam it over his head

He falls down

And

My sister and brother and mother are screaming: *(Does a voice)* "NO DOUGRAY—STOP!"

(Pause. Becomes self:)

I just kept hitting him

There was even a GRACE in the way I was hitting him

Something *(Slight pause)* / CLEAN / it was like a PURIFICATION.

(Beat.)

He passed out from the beating and the booze.

(Beat.)

I left that night

Never went back

I went to Jackson, Tennessee

Just hopped this bus

And

Got there

Found a shelter

Stayed there for a while

Got a job quickly working with a plumber

Moved out of the shelter

And

Found a place to live in Henderson

And

I got my GED

And

Went to college—University of Tennessee to study business

And

Got my degree.

(Beat.)

I did this coming from NOTHING.

(Pause.)

No one gave me anything. I did it all myself.

I bought my first house in Henderson—which I still own.

(Pause.)

I moved to St. Louis in 2010

I moved there because I could buy more property cheaper than in Henderson

And

Also

I was ready for a change

I live in Tower Grove.

And

I met a great woman

Married her

And

We have two great sons—aged four and five

And

At the time / it was mixed—with mostly blacks

But

Since

Then

It's changed—become mostly white

But

There are a lot of gays . . . *(Voice trails off)*

(Beat.)

Businesses are popping up all over the place

More housing

And

A lot have taken the buyouts and also many who did NOT own their homes.

(Pause. Proudly:)

I own my home

And

I also own two houses in Ferguson

One on Fargo Drive

And

Another on Gage near West Florissant.

(Pause.)

It is the black part of town

I rent to blacks

And

They pay me

They know to pay me on time.

(Pause.)

I see a lot of black boys acting like hoodlums

Getting high

Busting windows

Hanging around with their pants sagging over their butts blasting that damn rap music

Their hair uncombed and wild

Calling EACH OTHER "nigger" all the time

Saying: *(Mocks)* "Yo nigga / MY nigga / nigga . . ."

(Speaks normally:)

But

If a white person calls them that / they get mad

DAEL ORLANDERSMITH

They HATE the word

They've said: *(Sarcastically)* "The white man" called them that

And

They hate it

But

Yet they call each other that

And

The rap music is filled with it!

(Pause.)

Hypocrites!

It will change

Eventually it will change

That's the way real estate is.

(Beat.)

You have to think ahead

Be a visionary of sorts . . .

These people will disappear

And

Be replaced by other people

White people.

(Beat.)

I go to Ferguson all the time to check on my houses

And

They KNOW not to mess with my houses

And

They KNOW that I've ALSO got friends on the police force

They ALSO know I don't come alone.

(Points to his bag.)

I do come packing

And

Will shoot to kill

Because

You may have to—

You may have to KILL

It is your right to KILL if someone attacks you

And

These black bastards will do it

Like Michael Brown did.

No one is talking about how Darren Wilson had to defend himself

Darren's WHITE so OF COURSE it's his fault

They're all saying how Michael Brown tried to run away and how

Darren Wilson shot him in the back.

But

There is no evidence about him being shot in the back

And

They're scared of what the Black Leaders like that APE Al Sharpton will come

Down here and say.

(Beat.)

Ferguson can be great

And

I think with time—when all this mess is out of the way—it will be . . .

There's a great Italian restaurant there

And

A real nice wine bar

And

There's a great soul food place owned by blacks

A BLACK family owns this place

THIS BLACK family WORKS

WORKS hard

And

Prospers

And

Which means the REST of them can do that too

This family doesn't scream "white man this" / "white man that" . . .

(Beat.)

My oldest son Jesse and I were in the soul food restaurant

And

He was standing outside waiting for me as I was paying my check

And

I heard him scream: *(Does voice)* "STOP!"

(Becomes self:)

And

There were some kids—a little older about seven—standing around him / surrounding him / laughing, and there was the one kid who was about Jesse's age

They were all BLACK

And

The older ones made the young one punch Jesse

And

Then they said: *(Does a voice)* "That's for Michael Brown, man."

(Becomes self:)

And

Another one said: *(Does voice)* "Yeah hit him again for what Darren Wilson did to Mike Mike."

(Becomes self. Sarcastically:)

What the hell is that?

(Does voice:)

"Mike Mike."

(Becomes self:)

Stupid names THEY call each other

(Does voice:)

"Mike / Mike."

(Becomes self:)

Jesse ran to me

He ran to me

And

Grabbed me around the waist

And

Those little black bastards were bold enough to stand there pointing

Laughing.

(Quiet, but livid, powerful:)

They stood there laughing / pointing.

(Beat.)

I pushed Jesse away from me

I pushed him away and said: *(As if to him)* "Jesse go over there and beat him / beat that NIGGER / punch him as hard as you can

And

Keep punching him

Keep on . . ."

(Back to audience:)

And

Jesse said: *(Does him)* "No Daddy / NO / PLEASE!"

(Becomes self:)

And

I said: *(To him)* "Go over there NOW and hit that NIGGER back."

(Back to audience:)

And

I said it LOUD enough for everyone to hear me

And

I didn't care WHO heard me

And

Jesse said: *(Does him)* "Daddy what is that? A nigger / I don't know what that is!"

(Becomes self:)

And

I said: *(To son, pointing toward the gang of kids)* "THEM—that BOY that hit you / those DARK PEOPLE / those EVIL people are NIGGERS / now go and HIT HIM BACK NOW!"

(Back to audience:)

And

I looked down at Jesse

He was crying

His little body was shaking.

(Beat.)

I bent down and really looked him in the eye and said: *(As if to Jesse)* "You WILL do it Jesse / you will NOT let anyone hit you / you will not act like some queer / you go and you hit that NIGGER back right now / if you don't / I'll whip you in front of all these people / I mean it / I'll whip YOU in front of ALL OF THEM!"

(Back to audience:)

And

He ran towards them

He ran towards them SCREAMING

The SCREAM he let out was terrifying

His body SHOOK with Anger

DETERMINATION

He was only five

But

In that moment / he was thirty-five

And

He came at THEM

CHARGED at THEM

And

The look on their faces

THEY were afraid

Those little black bastards were afraid

And

Jesse hit the boy with such force

And

He hit some of the older boys too

And

By now there was a crowd

And

I stood there

Stood there holding my bag

My bag that held my gun

You know as I stood there watching the fight / I thought about the fight I had with my father and how I thought it would purify me and in the entire world

THEN

I thought of that movie *Schindler's List*.

There's a part in there where Amon Goeth goes down a line shooting Jews for stealing a chicken

He just goes down this line shooting these kikes

As I stood in Ferguson looking at those niggers staring me down

Rather

TRYING to stare me down—because I looked RIGHT back at them—this image came to me . . .

The image that came to me was Me and Amon Goeth and Darren Wilson lining all of them up right on West Florissant Avenue and gunning them down

In my head—the precision—perfect

Me and Darren and Amon would just line those bastards up

Line those BLACK bastards up

And

Slowly lift our guns—rifles actually

Looking into the rifles

Making sure the angles were right

And

Then

Begin to shoot

And

Keep shooting / keep shooting

Until

They all fall

DAEL ORLANDERSMITH

And

After all their blood has been spilled / there will be a great storm

A great rain storm making it all clean

Making the town clean

Making Ferguson clean like it must have been once

Clean

White

Purified

Like it must have been once

And

Will be again

Clean

Pure

(Pause.)

White.

(The lights fade on Dougray.)

PAUL

The lights come up on Paul Thompson: black, seventeen, high school student. Talks to audience:

PAUL

I'm not gonna live in fear / I just won't give into it. I do get afraid / I mean sometimes these cops around here / they mess with you for no reason . . .

(Pause.)

I live in the Canfield Apartments and I see what goes on

I stay to myself mostly

Or

When I go somewhere / I go to visit friends in Normandy

Or

St. Louis

Or

U City

And

yeah

some of my friends are white

and

they ARE my friends just like the black ones are.

(Beat.)

I got one more year

And

Then

I'm going to college in Berkeley, California

I want to study art history

I can't paint—I've tried so I figure I can learn about how it's done

Where it came from

And

I watched some of the kids I'm in school with paint

The WAY they paint

The way their wrists move—it's like liquid

It seems to me like their movements / the way they paint

is like the actual PAINT itself

The way their hands and arms move are liquid

But

Man I can't do that!

My painting is pathetic

So

I'll study the history—which I love doing.

(Pause.)

I love knowing about how things came to be

History is really interesting

I'm not big into basketball

I mean I can play ball

But

Just don't care for it.

(Beat.)

I go to McCluer High School and take art history at Flo Valley

A lot of us are college bound

Not ALL of us are into getting high

Not ALL of us are like that

Not all black dudes are into that

I mean it's common sense

There are good people and bad people

And

I can talk to my friends about this

I can talk to all my friends—black and white about this

And

The whole Michael Brown thing—

(Pause.)

I didn't know Michael Brown

Or

"Mike Mike" as people called him

I mean I seen him around

And

We'd nod at each other and say "hey"

But

That was about it.

(Pause.)

Like I said / I live in the Canfield Apartments—just like Michael Brown did.

You know if you look at a housing project

Or low-income apartments like Canfield—

I mean if you really look at it—it looks just like a prison

It really does look like a prison

And

Sometimes

it feels like that too

Feels just like a prison

There is something that's just—I dunno—DEFEATED there

It feels DEFEATED.

(Beat.)

And

When I go back there after school or after hanging out with my friends . . . *(Voice trails off)*

I hate it

I really hate living there

I mean there ARE good people that live there

Hardworking people who just don't have money—the working poor

There are GOOD hardworking black people

Like my parents

And

They do the best they can

I love them for that

And

They want the best for me

And

They know I really want to leave

And

Encourage me to do so.

(Pause.)

But

There were and still are a lot of guys in Canfield that cause trouble

And

I know for a fact that police didn't want to see the difference between the two

I know from personal experience.

(Beat.)

This one day I didn't take the bus home

A friend's father gave me a ride home from school

And

As

I was walking towards the house / I had both arms filled with books

Art books about da Vinci, Elizabeth Catlett, Romare Bearden

And

This policeman came up

And

He was white

and

he Stopped me

and

I was so scared

I was so scared that I thought I was gonna wet myself

I really thought I was gonna wet myself

And

The cop came up to me chewing gum smiling

Laughing almost

He could see how scared I was

And

He stops right in front of me saying: *(Does him)* "Where you get those books from boy?"

(Becomes self:)

I said: *(As if to him)* "School / I got the books from school."

(Back to audience:)

And

Then

The cop says: *(Does him)* "How do I know you didn't steal those books?"

(Becomes self:)

And

I said to him: *(As if to him)* "Sir, I don't steal but if I were a thief / do you really think I would risk MY life or jail for a BOOK? / A BOOK about Leonardo da Vinci?"

(Back to audience:)

And

The policeman fidgeted

I could tell he felt real stupid

Real stupid

And we stood there staring at each other for a minute and I was scared

I didn't know what he was going to do.

Then

He drove off

Some dudes were hanging around and saw what happened

And

They laughed

And said: *(As if to Paul)* "Yo Paul / you tole that cracker cop off man / you told him off real good / you an awright nigga."

(Back to audience:)

That incident made me cool with some people

Some of those guys even wanted to hang with me

But

I kept my distance

I just keep going

Keep minding my business.

(Beat.)

Every day I pass that shrine to Michael Brown

I pass it every day

Every single day

And

I think that could be me

That really could have been me

That could have been my blood flowing on this street

And

I think

I got one more year to get out

Just One more year

Please god / let me get out

Just let me get out

Please god—don't let that happen to me.

(The lights fade on Paul.)

EDNA

The lights come up on Edna Lewis: black, late fifties/early sixties, a universalist minister. Talks to audience:

EDNA

I've always believed in God

And

I have always wanted to be a minster and serve God

I think HE—God—is wonderful

I think SHE—God—is stupendous

My thinking about God this way has caused me trouble.

I knew it just couldn't be the old wiseman with the beard hanging in the sky or the blond man with blue eyes / white skin and long hair

He—God—is everyone

She—God—is everyone

GOD

White

Black

Yellow

Red

Brown

And

LOVE is EVERYONE . . .

(Beat.)

I questioned ALL of this as a child

I knew there had to be more to it than the Old Testament

And

If God called upon women to honor him / how come all preachers
are men?

How come when a woman has her monthly that's considered a
curse?

How can a woman's flow / the flow of a woman be evil?

If a woman didn't flow / have her flow / there would be no life

I asked my parents these questions

And

Boy my father had a fit

My mother said to me: *(Does her)* "Edna / you must leave things the way they are."

(Becomes self:)

But

I knew there was a part of her that felt the same way.

(Beat.)

I was born and raised in Kentucky

And

As an adult / I lived in a few different places

San Francisco

New York

Chicago

And

Finally here

I love St. Louis

And

I live in Tower Grove South

I practice ministry—Universalist Ministry

Again

God—her

God—him

Shiva

Kali

Buddha

Mohammed

Jehovah

Allah

Creator

It's about ALL of it.

(Beat.)

Love cannot be limited you know . . . *(Pause)* At one point I was
with a woman / I told my parents about this and they had a fit.

I explained: *(As if to them)* "God brought this incredible good person to me who happens to be a woman / this great person who too
loves GOD."

(Back to audience:)

And before I could finish / my mother cut me off saying: *(Does her)* "Don't you DARE bring the Lord into this." *(As her father)* "Don't come here again / don't call."

(Pause. Becomes self:)

We didn't speak for five years . . . my god how painful that was

And

Alice—my lover at the time—said: *(Does her)* "Don't give up on them / send letters / call . . ."

(Becomes self:)

And

They refused phone calls

And

They sent the letters back.

(Beat.)

Seven years ago / my dad passed

My mother called me

And

I asked her if the only reason why she contacted me was because she was afraid of being alone and she said: *(Does her)* "At first yes / but then I also realized that YOU are a good person and even though I don't agree with what you're doing / you are happy and doing God's work in your way . . ."

(Becomes self:)

And

That made me really happy to hear that.

(Beat.)

Alice and I broke up three years ago

And

Now I'm with a man

And *(Wryly)* my mother is ecstatic

But

She wasn't at first

My husband Kevin is white

And

Again

I explained to her about MY concept of love

GOD and love

And

Eventually she came around

And

She LOVES Kevin

And

Calls him "son."

She's been to the church where Kevin (who is also a minister) and I preach

And

She loves it

She said: *(Does her)* "I never seen so many different kinds of people in church before—it's wonderful."

(Beat. Becomes self:)

Living in Tower Grove South has been great

There used to be more black folks

And

Now

There are many gays

And

There are some other interracial couples

And

Lots of artists

But

Rent is going up

And

When that happens the rich come in . . .

Gentrification . . .

Poor folks get pushed out

Especially blacks

And

Now racial tension is super high.

(Beat.)

The Michael Brown case wears on me

hurts me

I've been to Ferguson

I've been to Canfield

I've prayed at Michael Brown's memorial spot

I've prayed for HIM.

(Pause.)

I've prayed for Darren Wilson.

(Beat.)

There was a protest at the county courthouse in Clayton

And

Kevin and I went

And

There were folks from Normandy, Kinloch, Berkeley, U City, North City, Ferguson—from CHICAGO—goodness—across the country there

And

There was MONUMENTAL anger.

(Beat.)

There was a day where the mostly black crowd were standing in front of predominately white policemen

In the eyes of the policemen

I saw those who wanted BLOOD

I saw those who wanted peace

And

I saw those who were afraid

Many of them YOUNG

Young men

Practically children

And

There were also some people from the National Guard

And

There were a lot of folk from the media there

And

In that crowd there were people who wanted peace

And

In that crowd there were others who wanted revenge

And

There were others who used the event to bring attention to themselves

People who wanted to sell books

And

CDs

People telling truth

People telling lies

And . . .

(Pause.)

Kevin and I did not go to protest

That's not what we wanted to do.

(Pause.)

I came with prayer

I came with GOD.

(Pause.)

I went to random people

And

Asked if they wanted to pray

And

You know many people did?

Many in the crowd did

And

Then

I went up to the police and the National Guard

And

The both of them were standing side by side

The young white policeman

And

The young black officer from the National Guard

And

I said to both of them: *(As if speaking to them)* "Gentlemen—and I do mean it when I call you GENTLE MEN because you were born Gentle—would the both of you like to Pray—not in the mushy way but in the HUMAN way / no matter what religion/color—none of that / just a Prayer for everyone and YOURSELVES and if not— would you let me Pray for you?"

(Back to audience:)

And

The young white officer / he was about twenty-three—not much younger than Darren Wilson I believe—looked at me

His lips quivered

His eyes were filled with tears

And

He said/stuttered: *(Does him)* "Ma'am . . . I can't . . . I'm on duty / I can't . . . I mean . . . I just can't . . ."

(Becomes self:)

And

I said: *(As if to him)* "That's okay / I can pray for you honey."

(Back to audience:)

And

Then

I spoke to the young black officer with the National Guard and asked him the same thing

And

He said: *(Does him)* "Please please pray for me / please do."

(Pause. Becomes self:)

And

I did

I prayed for both those young men

Some people got mad

But

That's how God speaks to me

That's how MY God speaks to me.

(The lights fade on Edna.)

LOUISA

Part Two

The lights come up on Louisa Hemphill. Talks to audience:

LOUISA

You know—and I hate saying this—I wonder about my faith / the foundation of my faith.

(Beat.)

There was an evening a few months back I was in Schnuck's in Ferguson and I heard a voice say—a woman's voice say: *(Does voice)* "I can forgive Darren Wilson / I know GOD has forgiven him / I hope he can forgive himself."

(Pause. Becomes self.)

I ran from my cart to the next aisle and saw Michael Brown, Sr. and his current wife talking to a man who I knew to be a Protester and the man just stood there looking at Mrs. Brown with his mouth open.

I did too

I just stood there

And

She then said: *(Does her)* "I did not give birth to Michael but he is STILL my son and I would say the same thing of my natural children."

(Pause. Becomes self:)

Michael Brown, Sr. said: *(Does him)* "I ain't there yet / I got work to do / I can't feel that way yet / just can't / one minute I feel nothing / the next minute I hate Darren Wilson / the next minute I'm mad at Mike . . . / I dunno . . ."

(Becomes self:)

I almost went over and said something

But

I could see THEY were trying

Trying to hold on

They wanted to go on with their shopping

But

Folks kept coming up to them

They wanted PEACE.

(Pause.)

I've ALWAYS considered myself a God-fearing woman

But

That young girl—Mrs. Brown—has more God in her that I EVER could.

(Pause.)

I had to and still have to search my heart on this.

(Pause.)

At church today / I thought, Michael, you were so close / close to getting out / to leaving / BECOMING SOMEONE / YOU ARE NOT A NIGGER / YOU WERE SO CLOSE! WHY would you put yourself between a WHITE man and a GUN?

You could have gotten out, Michael

Crossed the Mississippi River

Gone

Up to

Chicago

Gone

East

Maybe New York

You could have gotten out

Gone past

Why didn't you let yourself get past the river.

(Beat.)

And

The other young man Darren Wilson

I thought: "Did you have to SHOOT him? / Did you really HAVE to shoot him and if so / why so many times / why did you have to SHOOT TO KILL?"

The HATRED I had for that boy—Darren Wilson

MY GOD the Hatred . . . *(Voice trails off)*

(Pause.)

I thought—and God forgive me—I thought: "Where is God?"

"Why God did you allow this to happen? Where were you?"

(Beat.)

I'm also an educator. Everyone in my family were teachers

My mother

My father

I've got an older sister—she taught high school math

And

I'm a retired English teacher

And

I think what values we teach our kids?

What society have we created?

I think of family values

What kind of family did Darren Wilson come from?

How was he raised?

How was he made to feel about himself?

Was he also afraid?

He is not much older than Michael was

Did he JUST fire and not THINK?

And

Now does he THINK about it?

Does it play over and over in his mind / soul?

And

If it doesn't

If he DOES NOT care /

what created HIS hardness?

What made him so hard?

What / who made him so hard?

What was HIS legacy?

And

I think of Michael Brown and myself. / What we were taught.

I think of OUR legacy.

(Pause.)

MY god

The things we are taught. The things we remember. All the things we can't stop knowing / can't stop knowing in our bones.

(The lights fade on Louisa.)

POET/PLAYWRIGHT

The lights come up on the Poet/Playwright, who recites a poem to the audience:

POET/PLAYWRIGHT

Every night I see their eyes / I hear the voices of

Frightened boys

Men

Dark boys / men

EVERYWHERE

Dark boys

White boys / men

Roaming

Streets—going nowhere

Boys

Boys

Trying to get somewhere boys

But don't know how

Because

Boys are told

To be hard—boys

Be rough—boys

Don't cry—boys

Black boys

B-boys / backslide

Back beat

Bull-whipped

Tired of the bullshit boys

Be-bop boys

with

Broken hearts

Dodging slaps

Bullets planned

and

Random

White boys

Ravaged by stinging WASP lies

Can

Smell the blue blood curdling

Are

Now

Skinned

Skinless

Prowling

Praying for God

or

Some such man

Seemingly

Untouchable

Unreachable

Neither boy

Able to

Sleep

Rest

Neither boy

Knowing how to take care

Being able to rest—boy

Be heard boy

Some say

Bad boy

Some say sad boy

Some say misunderstood boy

So

Silence the boy

Quiet the boy

Kill the boy

Punish the man

Boy

Man

Boy

Man

Black

White

Gun

Shoot

Black boy—down

White man—shoot

Both down

Both are down

Both are done

Done

Gone

Both gone

They are BOTH gone

and

Has the "we shall overcome"—come

and

Gone?

And

Has the wake-up call been answered

and

Deleted?

Maybe

Maybe so

but

There are those who STILL wake up

Arms

Hands

Outstretched

Saying words

Like:

MORE

NOT YET

BUT SOON

SOON

VERY SOON.